Hedgehogs

OUR WEIRD PETS

Melissa Raé Shofner

PowerKiDS
press.

New York

Published in 2018 by The Rosen Publishing Group, Inc.
29 East 21st Street, New York, NY 10010

First Edition

Editor: Melissa Raé Shofner
Book Design: Rachel Rising

Photo Credits: Cover, p. 1 Mr. SUTTIPON YAKHAM/Shutterstock.com; Cover versh/Shutterstock.com; p. 5 Zanna Holstova/Shutterstock.com; p. 7 Les Stocker/Oxford Scientific/Getty Images; p. 8 (pet food) Nenov Brothers Images/Shutterstock.com; p. 8 (mealworm) Kuttelvaserova Stuchelova/Shutterstock.com; pp. 9, 17, 22 Best dog photo/Shutterstock; p. 11 Tamara83/Shutterstock.com; p. 12 Ajintai/Shutterstock.com; p. 13 Elena11/Shutterstock.com; p. 15 © iStockphoto.com/MirasWonderland; p. 16 © iStockphoto.com/bazilfoto; p. 19 MaaDerLaa/Shutterstock.com; p. 20 © iStockphoto.com/GlobalP; p. 21 Dejan Dundjerski/Shutterstock.com.

Cataloging-in-Publication Data
Names: Shofner, Melissa Raé.
Title: Hedgehogs / Melissa Raé Shofner.
Description: New York : PowerKids Press, 2018. | Series: Our weird pets | Includes index.
Identifiers: ISBN 9781508154211 (pbk.) | ISBN 9781508154150 (library bound) | ISBN 9781508154037 (6 pack)
Subjects: LCSH: Hedgehogs as pets–Juvenile literature. | Hedgehogs–Juvenile literature.
Classification: LCC SF459.H43 S56 2018 | DDC 636.9'332–dc23

Manufactured in the United States of America

CPSIA Compliance Information: Batch #BS17PK: For Further Information contact Rosen Publishing, New York, New York at 1-800-237-9932

Contents

Happy Hedgies

When it comes to pets, you probably don't think about hedgehogs. But hedgies, as they're sometimes called, make great pets! They're about as smart as hamsters and take up about the same amount of space as guinea pigs. If you've ever thought of owning one of these other small pets, you may want to consider a hedgehog.

There are 16 different species, or kinds, of hedgehogs around the world. Some species make great pets, but others are best left in the wild.

PET FOOD FOR THOUGHT

The most common type of pet hedgehog is the African pygmy hedgehog.

African pygmy hedgehogs are usually about 5 to 8 inches (12.7 to 20.3 cm) long and weigh between 0.5 and 1.25 pounds (0.2 and 0.6 kg).

5

In the Wild

Hedgehogs live in many different **environments**. In the wild, hedgehogs live in deserts, forests, and even cities. They live throughout Asia, Europe, and Africa. Hedgehogs are mostly nocturnal, meaning they sleep during the day and are awake at night.

Some hedgehogs dig **burrows**. Others make nests out of leaves, grasses, and branches. Some hedgehog burrows can be up to 20 inches (50.8 cm) deep. Hedgehogs like to live alone, so you won't find a big family of adult hedgehogs living together.

PET FOOD FOR THOUGHT

In Asia, one type of hedgehog often uses burrows built by turtles, foxes, and other animals.

In the desert, hedgies hide between rocks and plants or dig into the sand to stay cool.

A Balanced Diet

Hedgehogs are insectivores, or animals that eat mostly insects. Don't worry about catching bugs, though. You can get food for your hedgehog at the pet store. Some pet stores sell food specially made for hedgehogs. Certain cat foods are also an option for your hedgehog's **diet**.

Fresh water should always be available for your pet to drink. Use a small, heavy bowl so your pet can't tip it over. Make sure to clean and refill the bowl regularly.

cat treats

mealworm

PET FOOD FOR THOUGHT

Like cats and dogs, hedgehogs love treats! They like crickets, mealworms, and cat or dog treats.

Your hedgie can eat certain fruits and vegetables as treats, but don't give them too many. Never give your pet dairy products. These aren't good for hedgehogs.

A Home for Your Hedgie

Your hedgehog's cage should be at least 4 feet by 2 feet (1.2 by 0.6 m) so it has room to play. Some hedgehogs can learn to use **litter** pans when they go to the bathroom, but others are messier.

Most of the time, you won't need to bathe your hedgehog. Most hedgehogs clean themselves by licking, scratching, and shaking. If you have a particularly messy hedgehog, you should clean it carefully so it doesn't get sick or start to smell.

PET
FOOD
FOR
THOUGHT

Hedgehogs usually live between three and eight years, but some can live up to ten years.

Like other pets, hedgehogs enjoy playing with toys. An exercise wheel will help keep them active.

Pokey Pets

The first thing you'll likely notice about hedgehogs is their pointy **quills**. When you first learn how to hold a hedgehog, its quills may poke you. It might feel like being poked by a cactus.

Your pet isn't trying to hurt you. It's just trying to stay safe. When attacked, hedgehogs curl up in a ball, making their quills stick out. This hurts predators and keeps them from attacking the hedgehog. When your hedgie becomes comfortable around you, it won't roll up and poke you as much.

cactus

PET FOOD FOR THOUGHT

Hedgehog quills are made of **keratin,** the same thing your hair and fingernails are made of.

When you first hold your hedgehog, you might want to wear gloves to avoid being poked by its quills.

Can You Have One?

In many places, hedgehogs are considered **exotic** pets. This means there might be laws or rules about whether you can own one. Hedgehogs are illegal to own as pets in many places, including Georgia, Pennsylvania, and California. You should check the laws in your area before buying a hedgie.

Pet hedgehogs usually do best alone. If you have more than one hedgie you should always keep them in separate cages. Two male hedgehogs in the same cage will almost always fight each other.

PET FOOD FOR THOUGHT

In the wild, an adult female hedgehog usually has four to seven babies once or twice a year.

Baby hedgehogs are called hoglets.

Not a hog!

Despite their name, hedgehogs are not related to hogs or pigs. Hedgehogs probably got their name because of their **foraging** methods. They search through **hedges** and other plants to find food. When doing this, hedgehogs sometimes grunt and sound like pigs.

Because of their appearance, some people think hedgehogs are related to porcupines. However, the only thing these two animals really have in common is their quills. Porcupines are **rodents**, but hedgehogs are not.

PET FOOD FOR THOUGHT

Hedgehogs can have up to 44 teeth. That's more teeth than people have!

Some people think a hedgehog's nose looks like a pig's nose. However, the "hog" part of their name most likely comes from the sound they make when looking for food.

Healthy Hedgehogs

Hedgehogs don't normally require shots or tests like other pets do. You should still take your hedgehog to a vet for a yearly checkup, though.

Hedgehogs can get mites. Mites are tiny creatures, similar to ticks, that **invade** another animal's body and can make it sick. If your hedgehog starts losing a lot of its quills or you see little white dots moving around on its body, it may have mites. You should take your pet to the vet right away.

PET FOOD FOR THOUGHT

Some small pets, such as mice and ferrets, can be smelly. Healthy hedgehogs shouldn't smell at all.

Most hedgehogs have between 3,000 and 5,000 quills.

Playful Pals

Hedgehogs can make great companions. Most hedgies are fairly easy to care for. If you take good care of yours, you'll have a friend for life! Many hedgehogs love playing with their owner. Just make sure you and an adult keep a close eye on your pet whenever you take it out of its cage.

Many hedgehogs enjoy running on wheels and playing in tunnels and **mazes**. Even a toilet-paper tube can make a fun toy for an active hedgehog!

PET FOOD FOR THOUGHT

Plastic pipes, which you can buy at stores that sell tools, make great tunnels for hedgehogs to play in.

Make sure an adult is around whenever you take your hedgehog out of its cage.

Hedgehog Care Fact Sheet

- Hedgehogs can eat insects, special hedgehog food, and cat food.
- Your pet's cage should be large enough that it has room to play.
- Clean your hedgie's litter pan and cage regularly.
- Hedgies love toys like exercise wheels and tunnels.
- Hold your hedgie gently to avoid being poked by its quills.
- Take your pet to the vet at least once a year.
- Don't keep more than one hedgehog in a cage.
- Make sure your hedgie always has fresh water.

Glossary

burrow: A hole an animal digs in the ground for shelter.

diet: The food and drink that an animal consumes.

environment: The conditions that surround a living thing and affect the way it lives.

exotic: From another country or place; out of the ordinary.

forage: To hunt or search for something, such as food.

hedge: A row of bushes often used as a boundary.

invade: To enter or take over.

keratin: A material that is found in human hair and nails and in animal fur, scales, and horns.

litter: Material used to absorb the waste of animals.

maze: A system of paths or tunnels in which it's easy to become lost.

quill: A long, sharp, thin spine.

rodent: A small, furry animal with large front teeth, such as a mouse or rat.

Index

Websites

Due to the changing nature of Internet links, PowerKids Press has developed an online
list of websites related to the subject of this book. This site is updated regularly. Please
use this link to access the list: www.powerkidslinks.com/owp/hedg